BENNY THE BLUE
AND THE
ABSENT SHOE

ISBN: 978-0-578-30820-3

Layout by: Kenmark Designs

Illustrated by: Zain Osundwa

First Edition 2021

BENNY THE BLUE AND THE ABSENT SHOE

Written By: Diedre Osundwa

Illustrated By: Zain Osundwa

2

What do I do?
Says Benny the Blue.
I've lost my shoe
And don't know what to do.

4

Did I leave it in the park
Under the swing I was on?
Is it on top of the slide?
Oh My! What if it's gone?

5

6

How Can I run
Or Jump in a puddle?
How can I go to mommy
And give her a cuddle?

What if my foot gets too hot
Where the pavement is sunny?
It will burn my toes
Which won't be funny!

Then I'll be a hopper.

No more running really fast.

Someone please find my shoe!

How long will this last?

Then it occurred...

Let me look in my room!

There could be a place.

I'll look in the corner.

In the empty space.

14

It started to become clear to me.

The last place I was in,

Was under all of my clothes

Right in my toy bin!

Hooray! Hooray!
There's my shoe!
Red and Yellow
With a hint of blue.

17

Now I can run really fast

I found my shoe

Finally at last!

I can run and jump in a puddle.

Then I can give mommy

A great big cuddle!

www.ingramcontent.com/pod-product-compliance
Lightning Source LLC
Chambersburg PA
CBHW042002100426
42813CB00019B/2959